BOTANICAL ART DESIGN
ADULT COLORING BOOK II

PLEASE VISIT OUR WEBSITE FOR MORE INFORMATION ON NEW DESIGNS, BOOKS AND AVAILABLE MATTED PRINTS AT
WWW.BOTANICALARTDESIGNS.COM

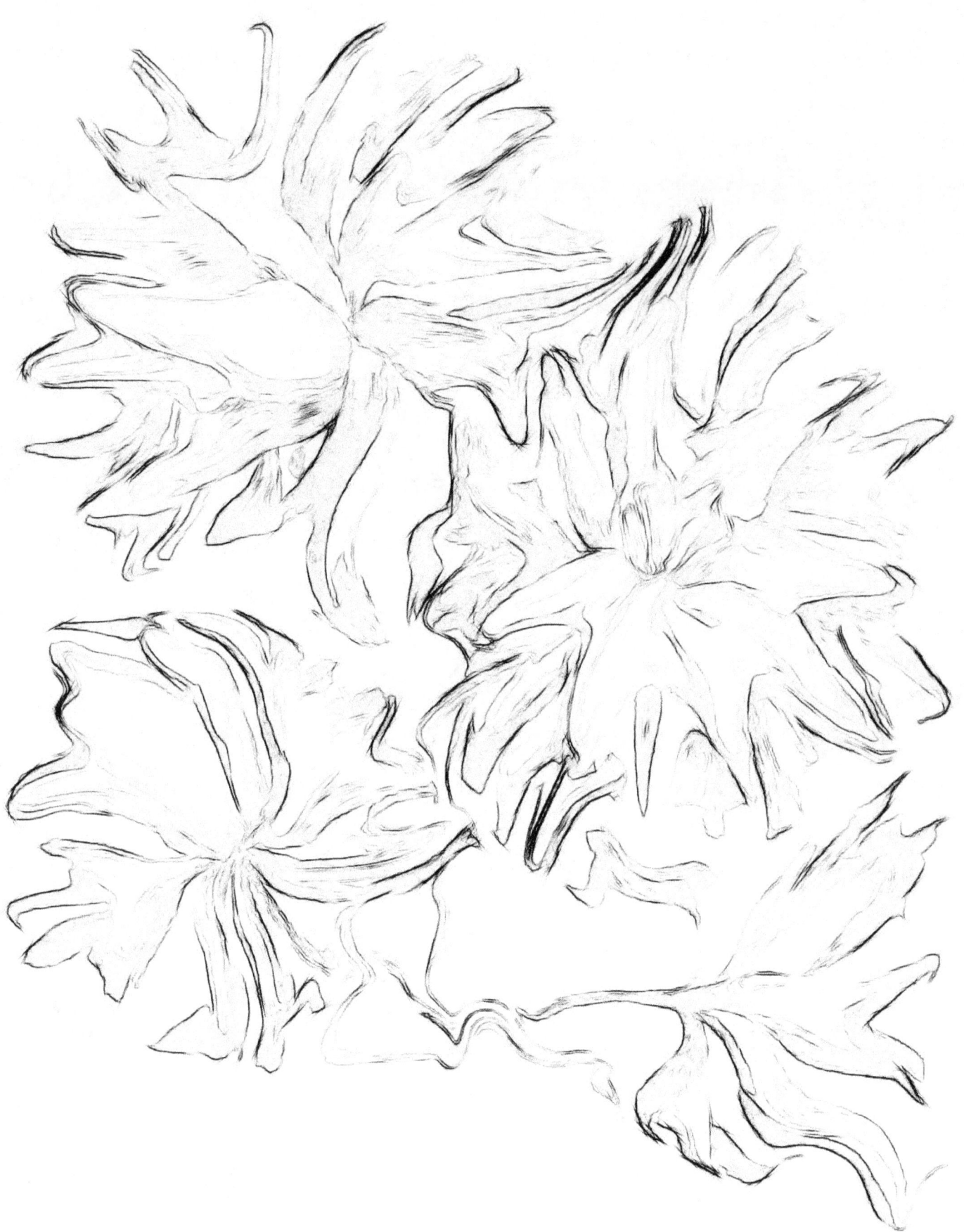

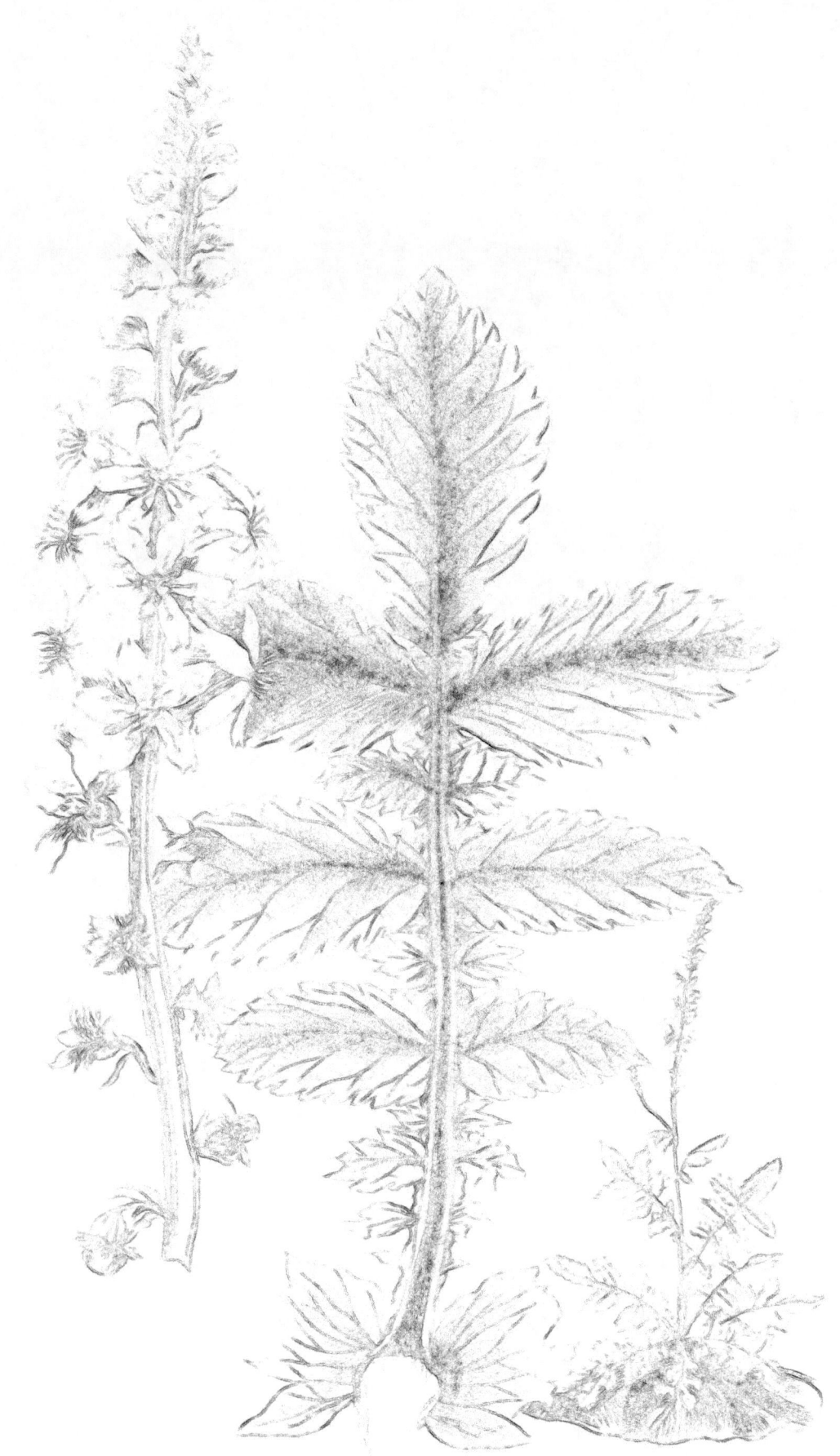

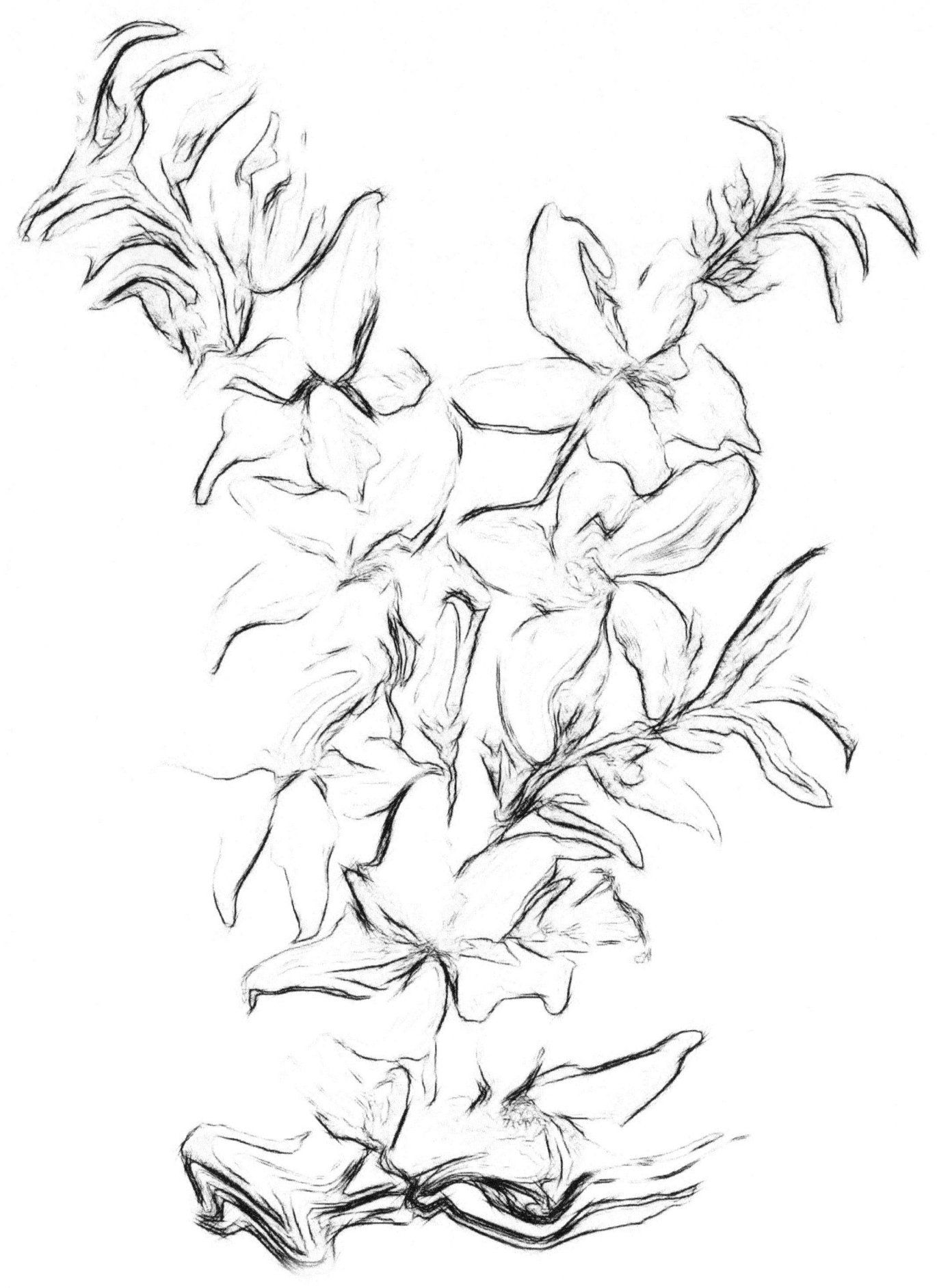

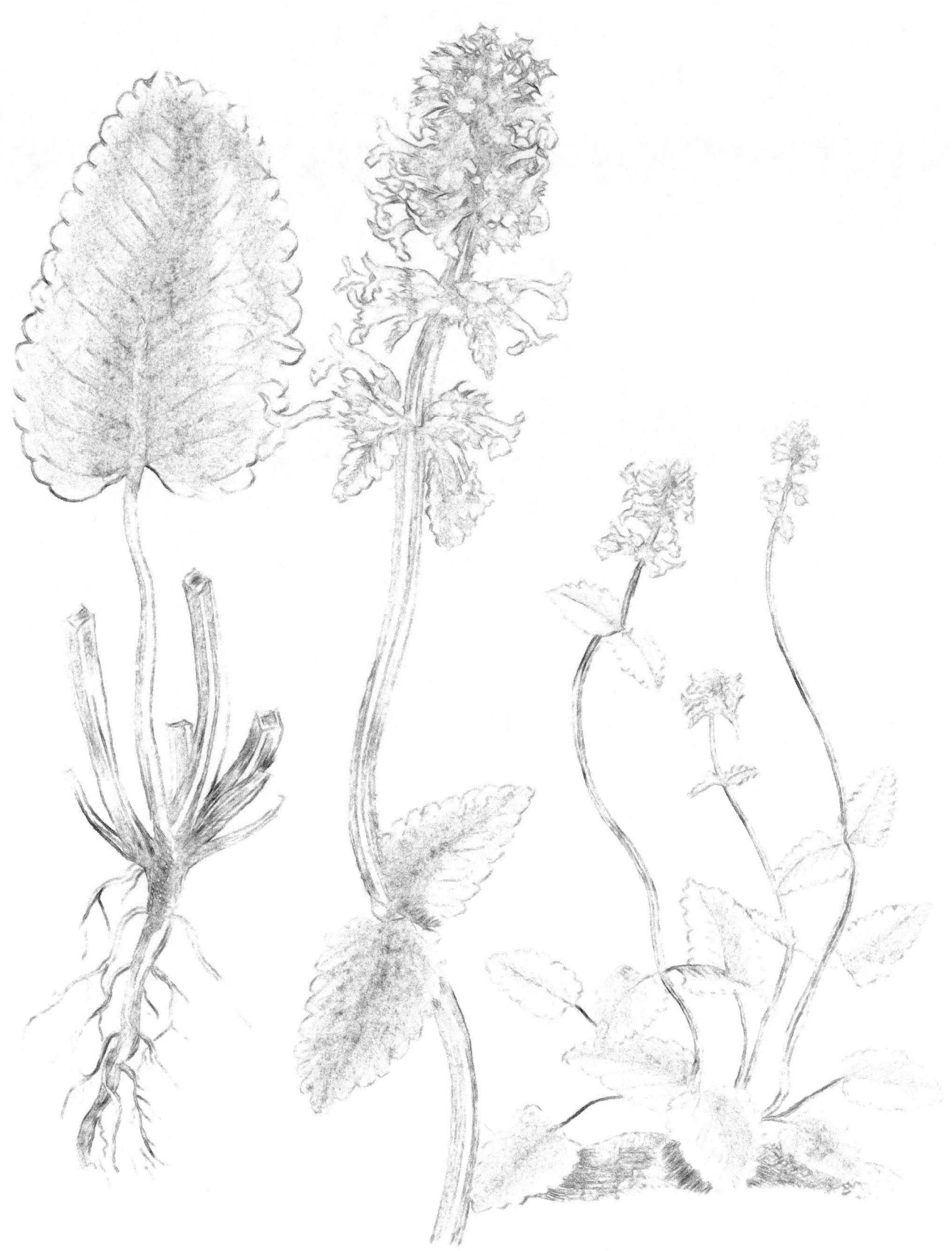

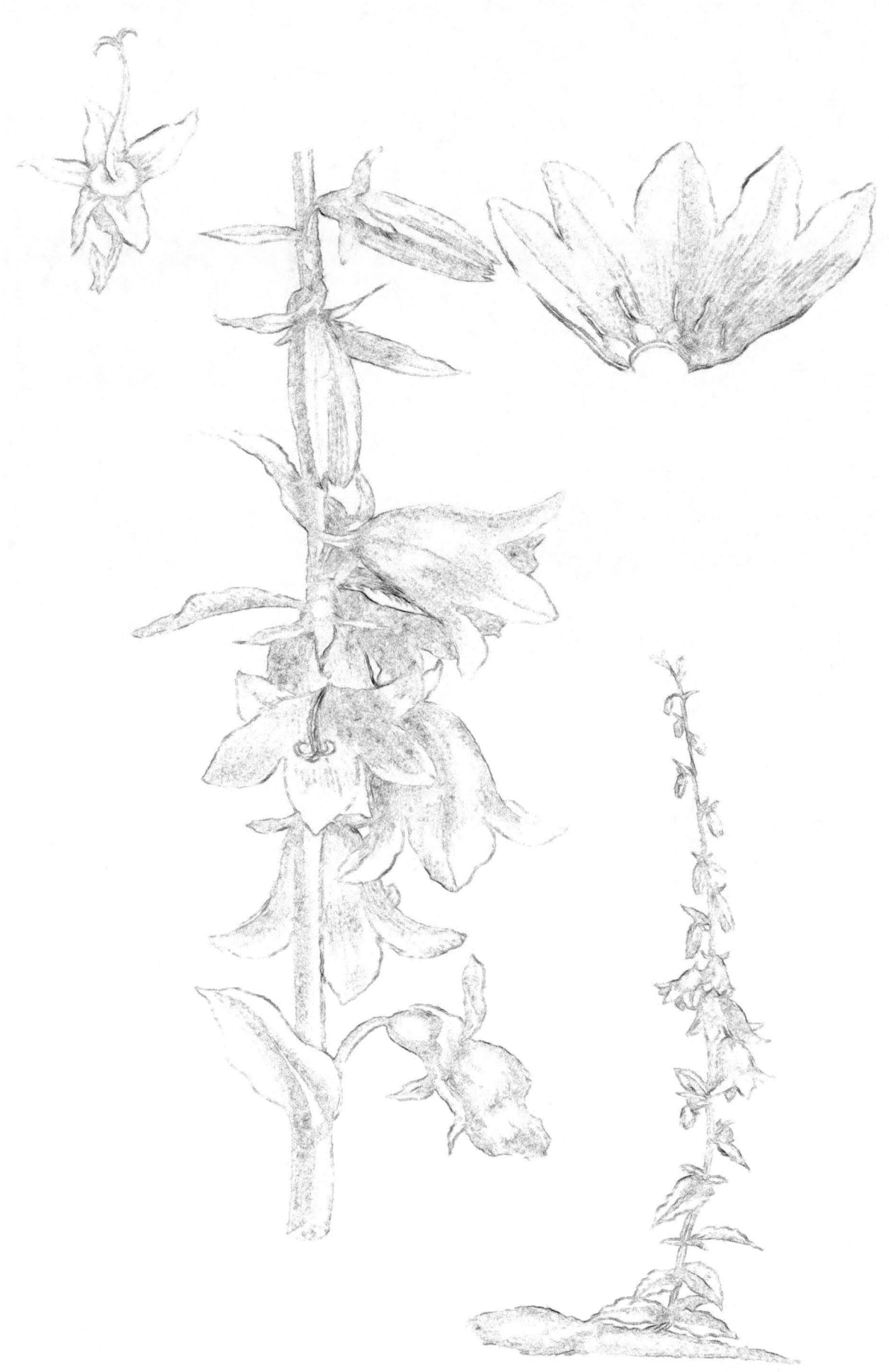

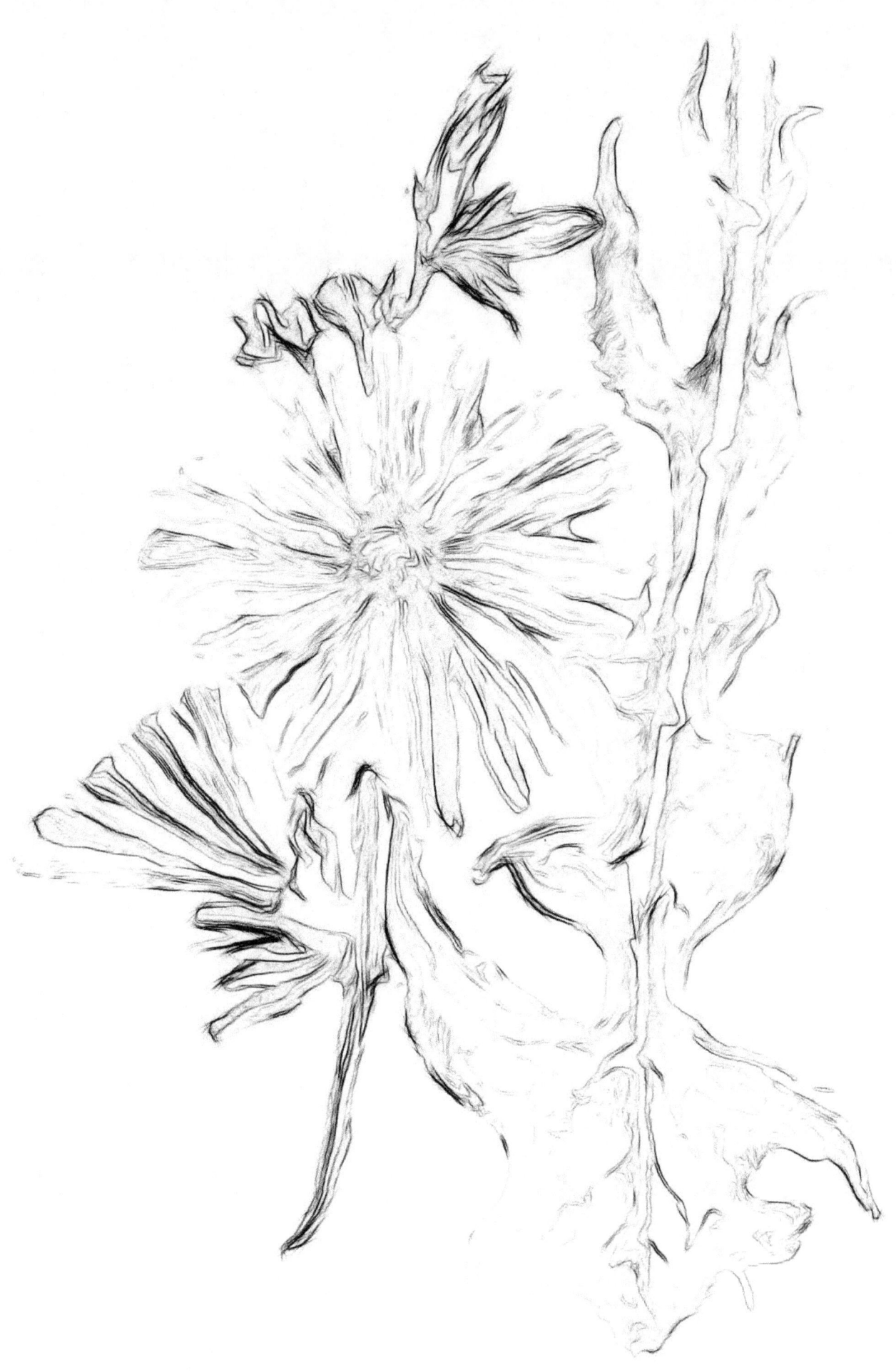

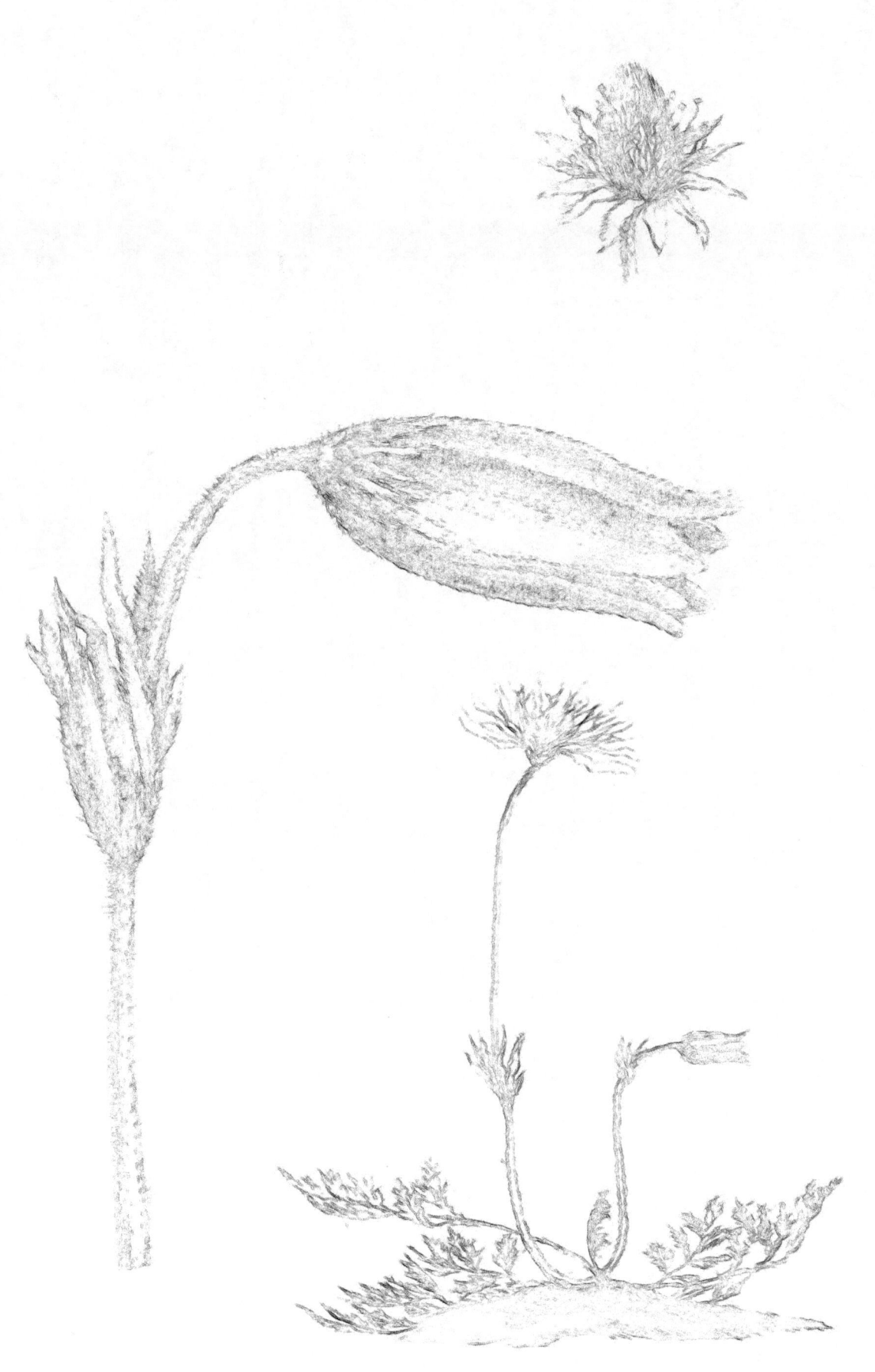

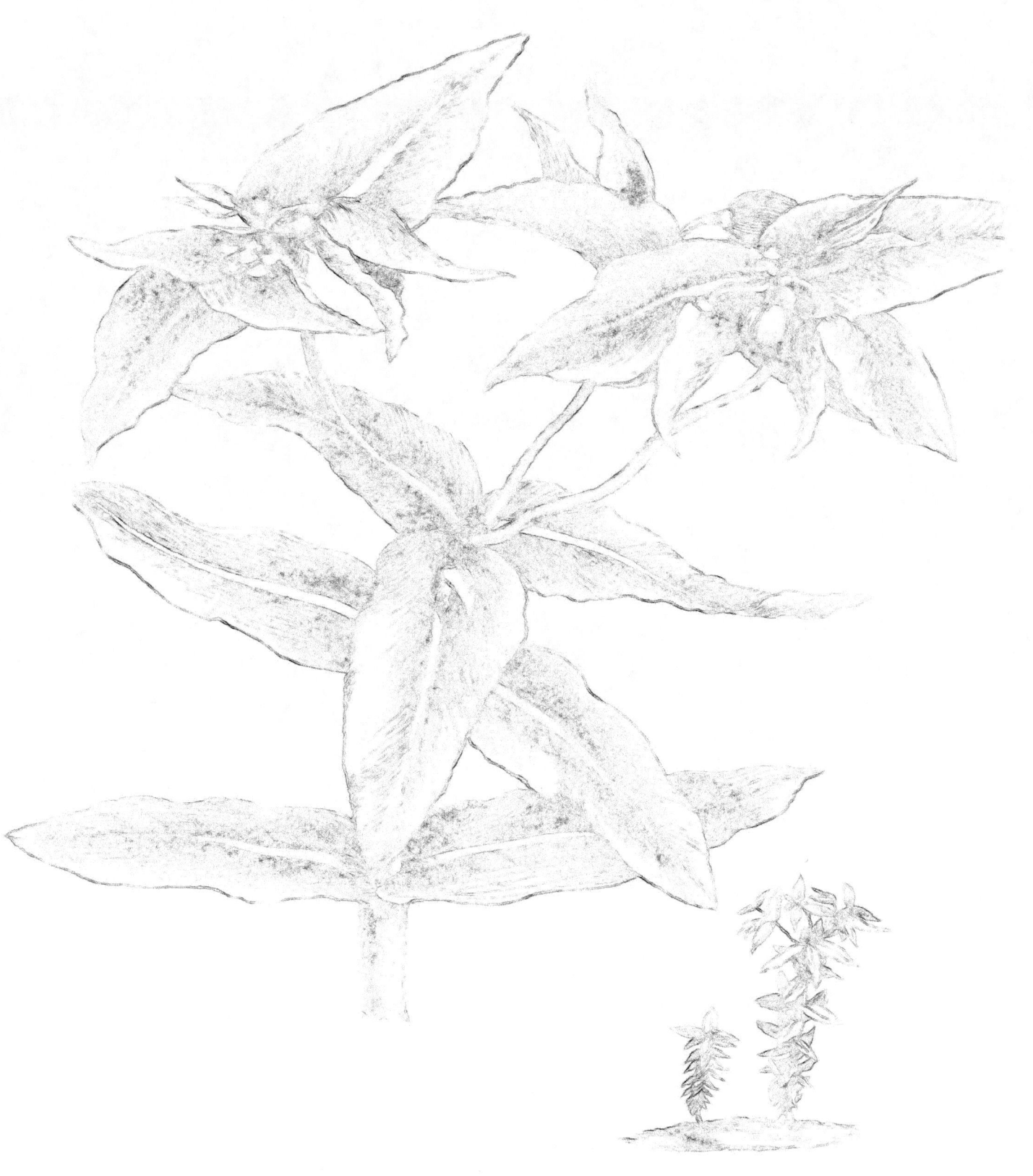

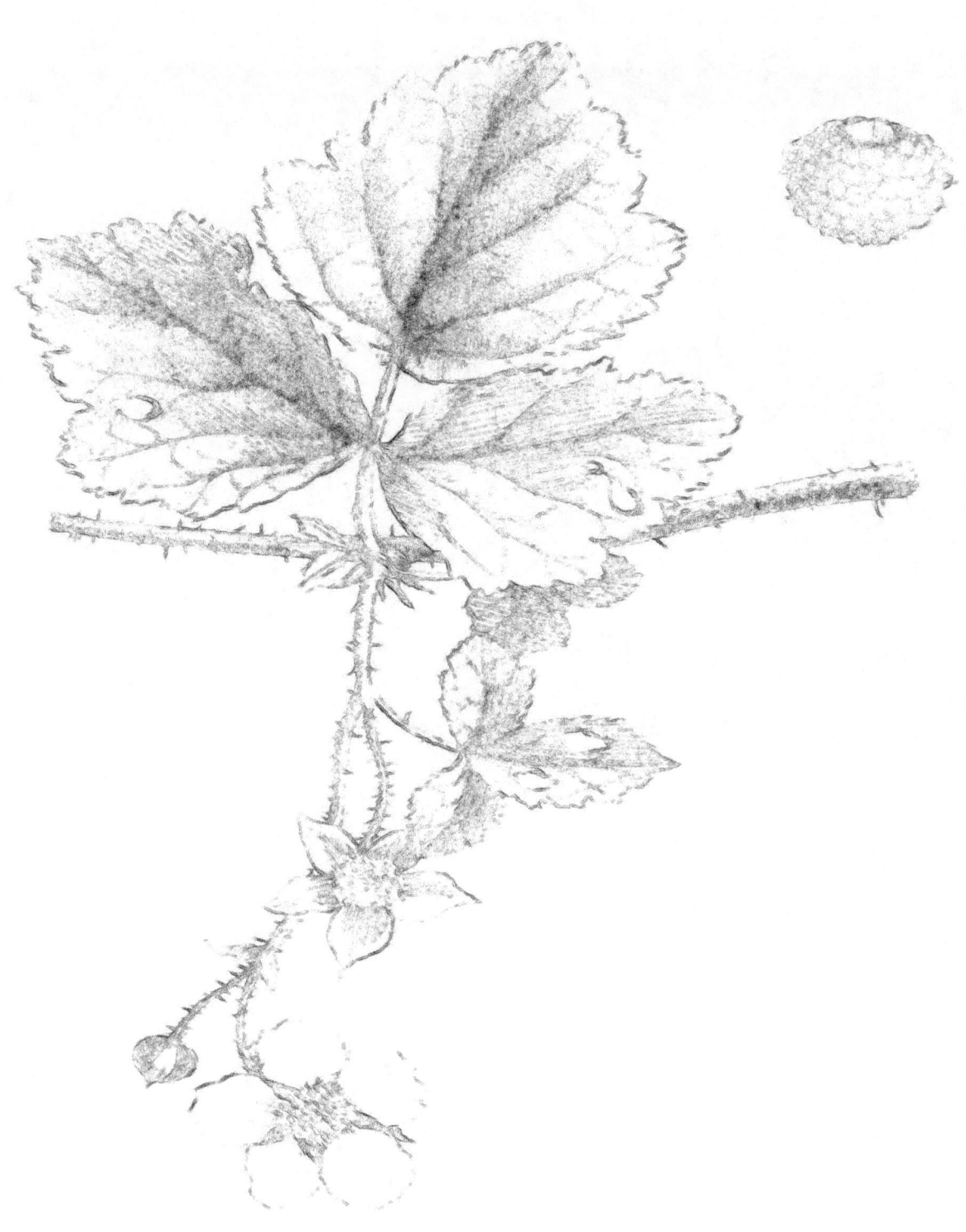

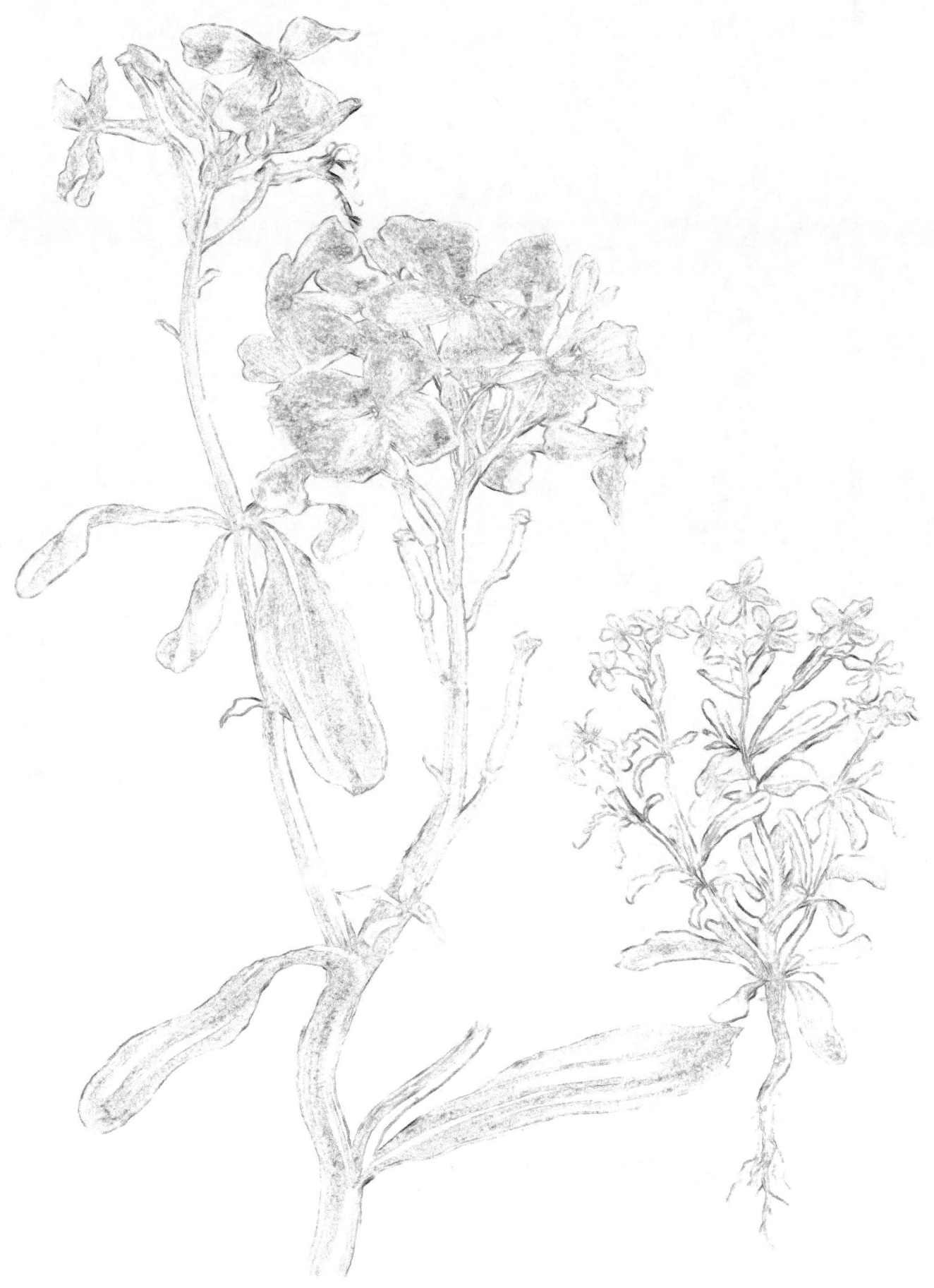

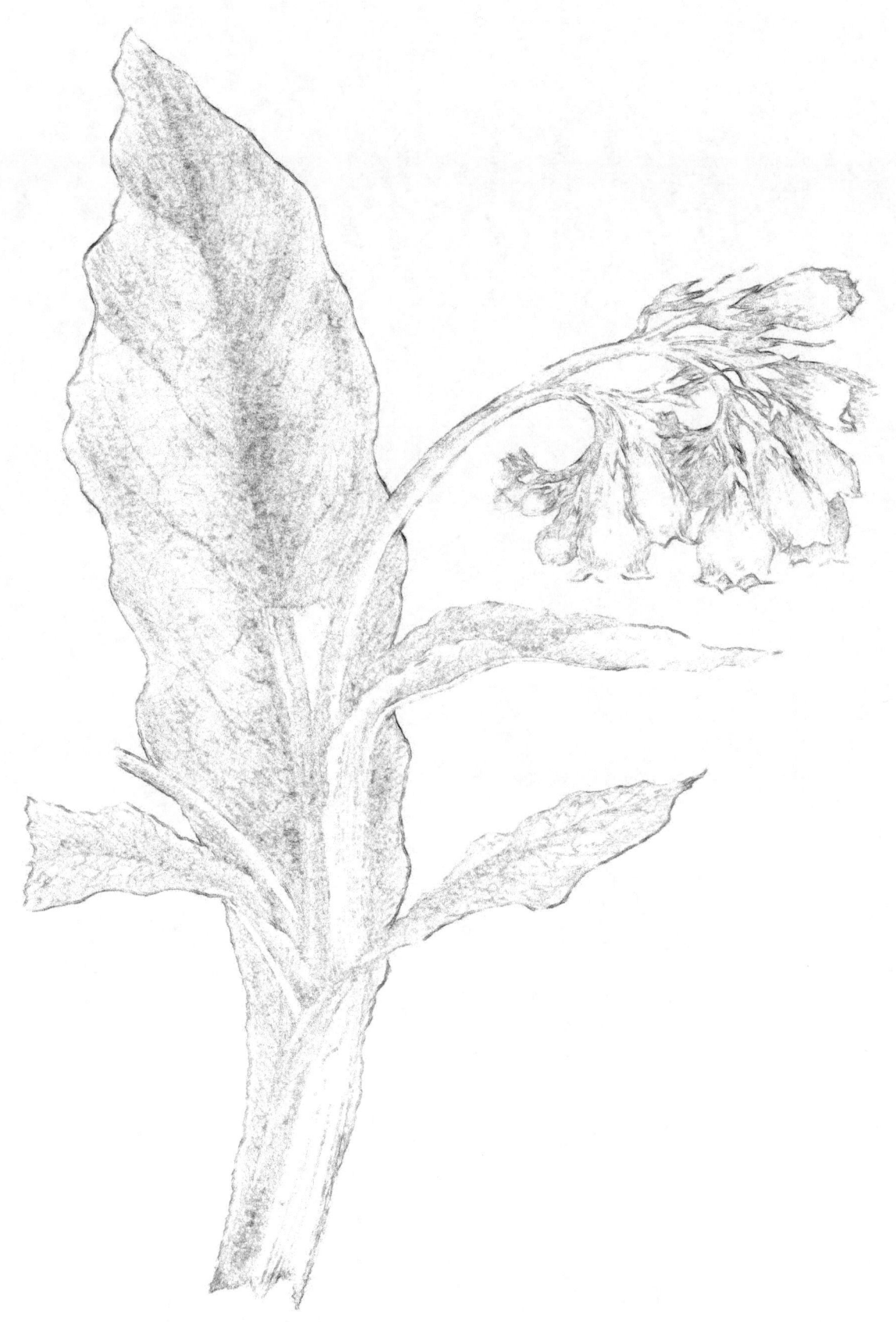

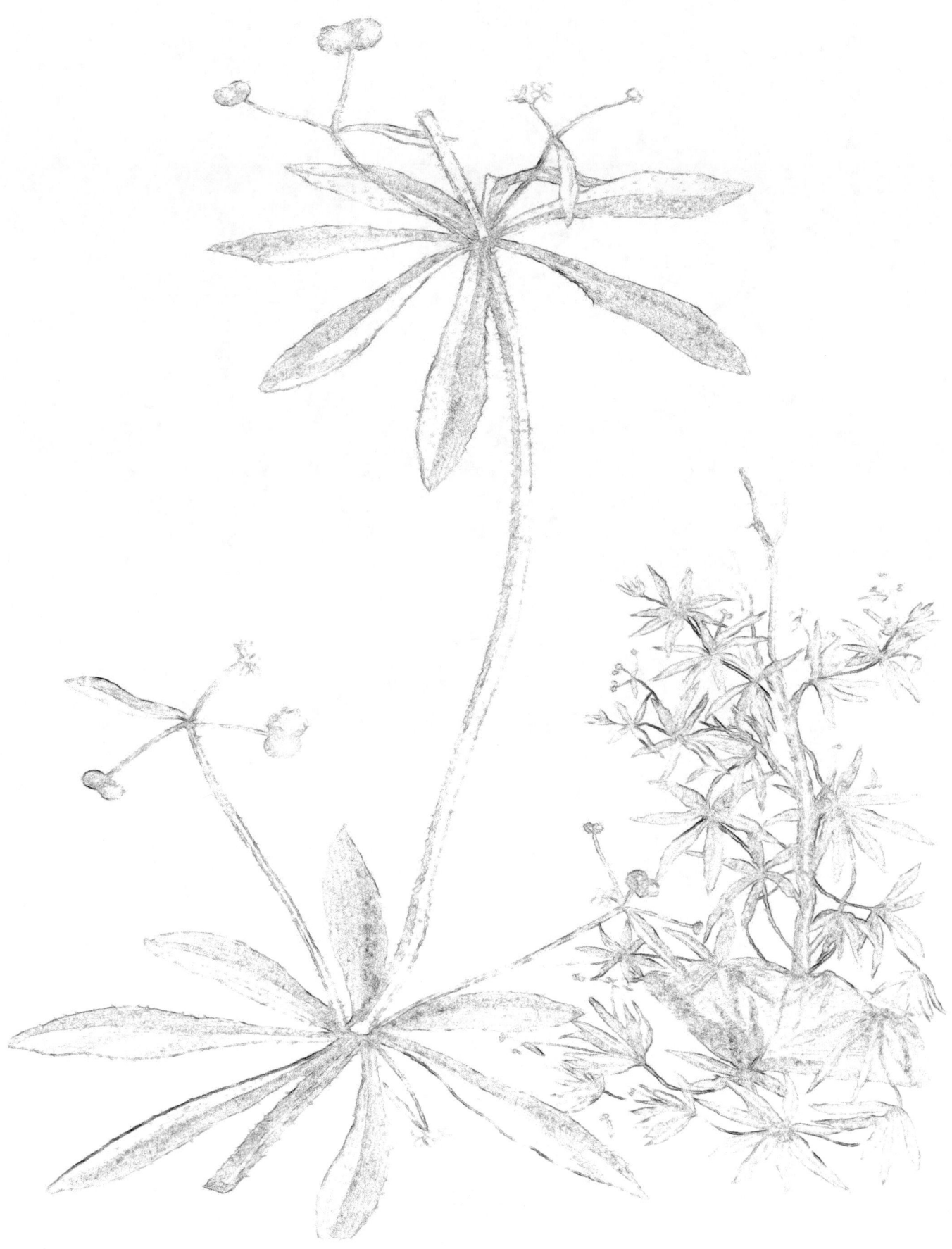

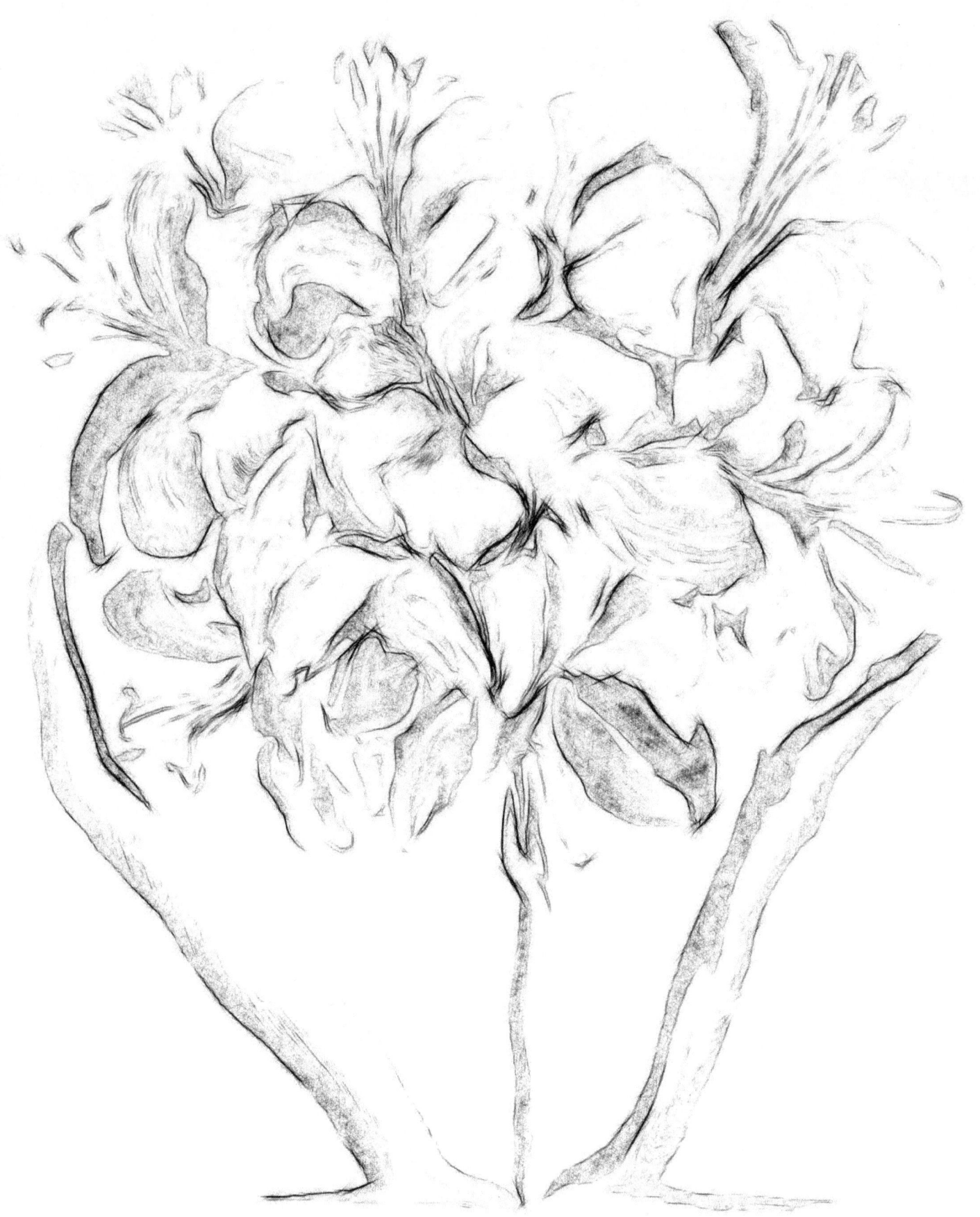

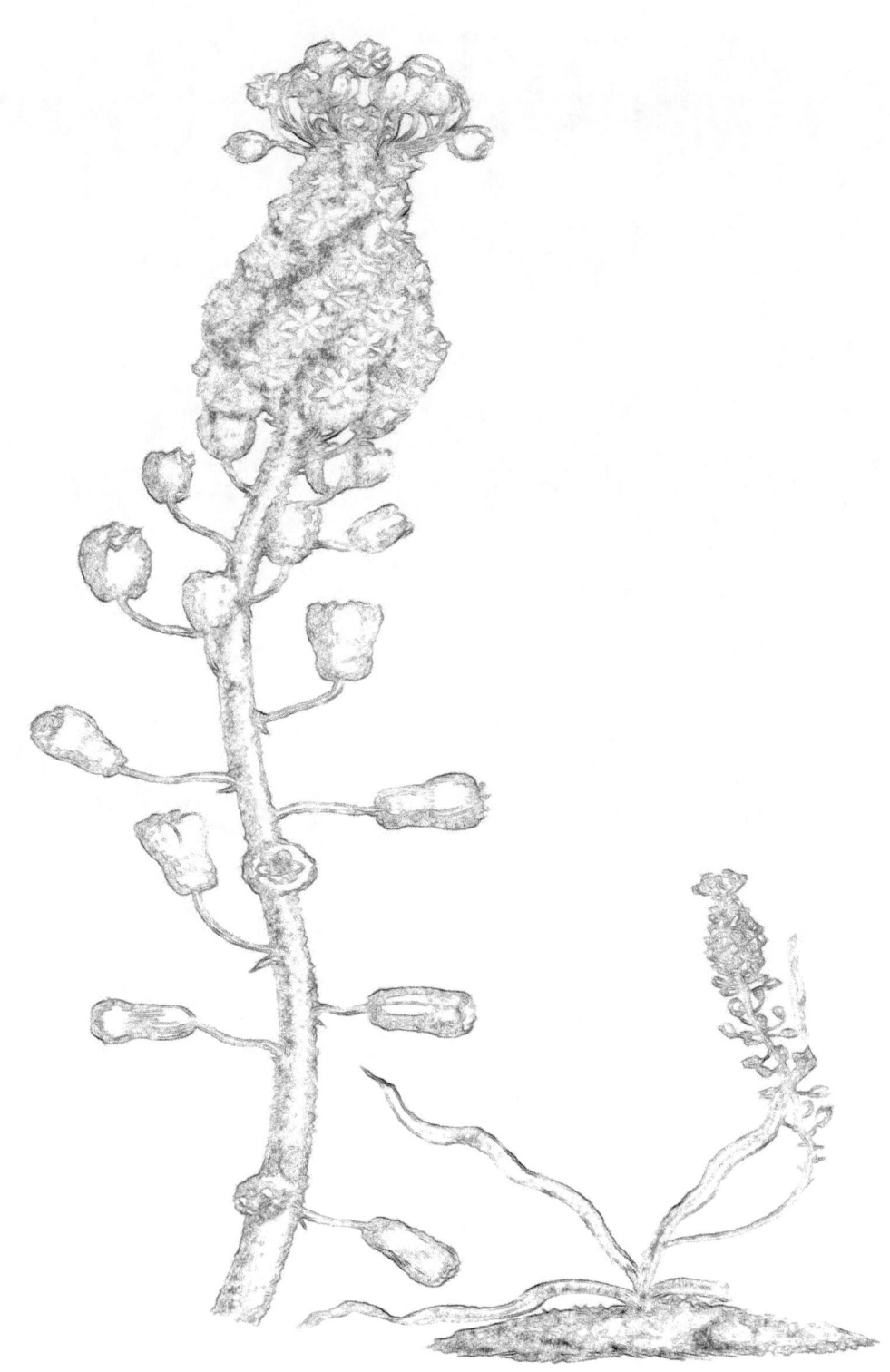

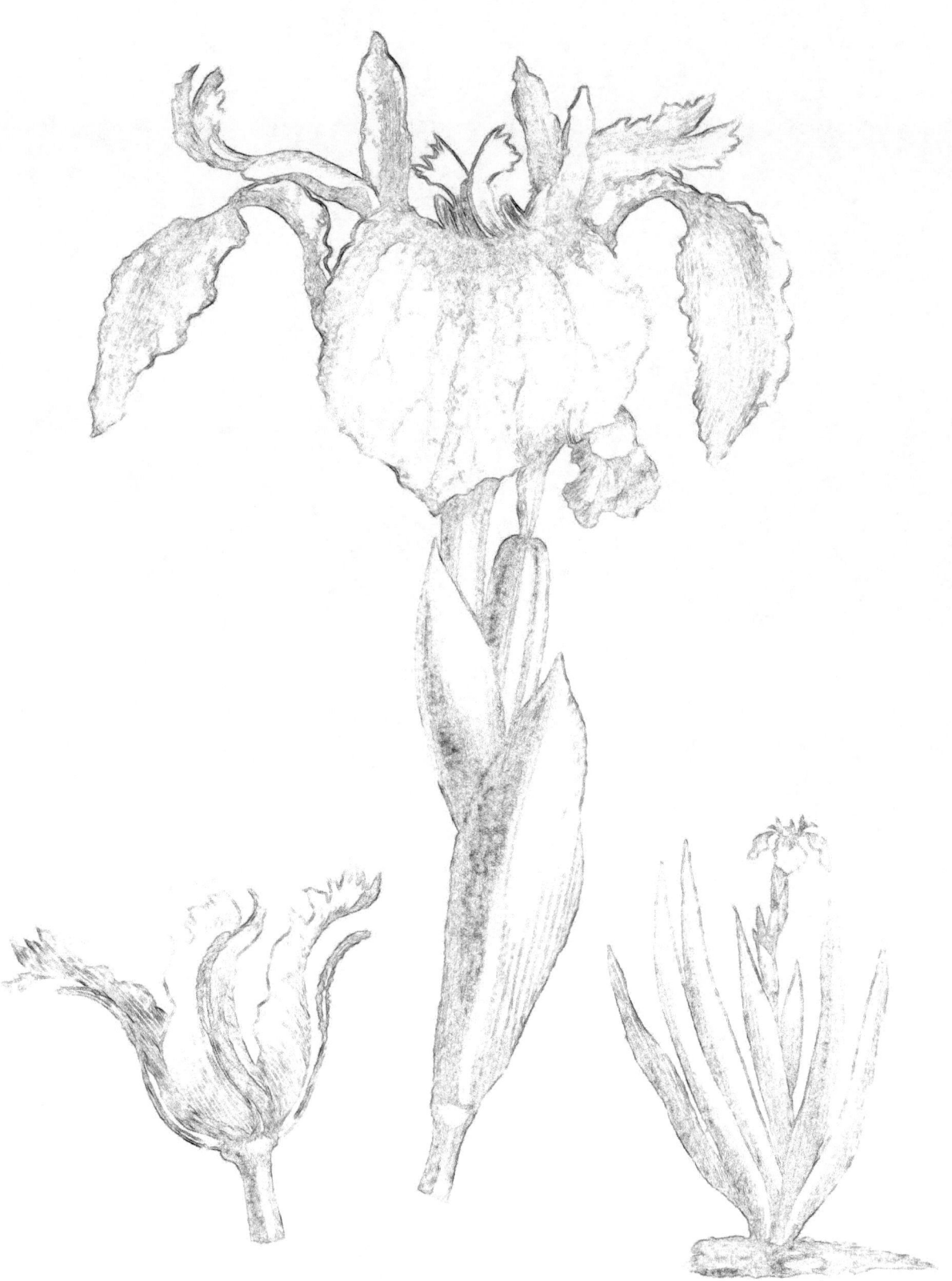

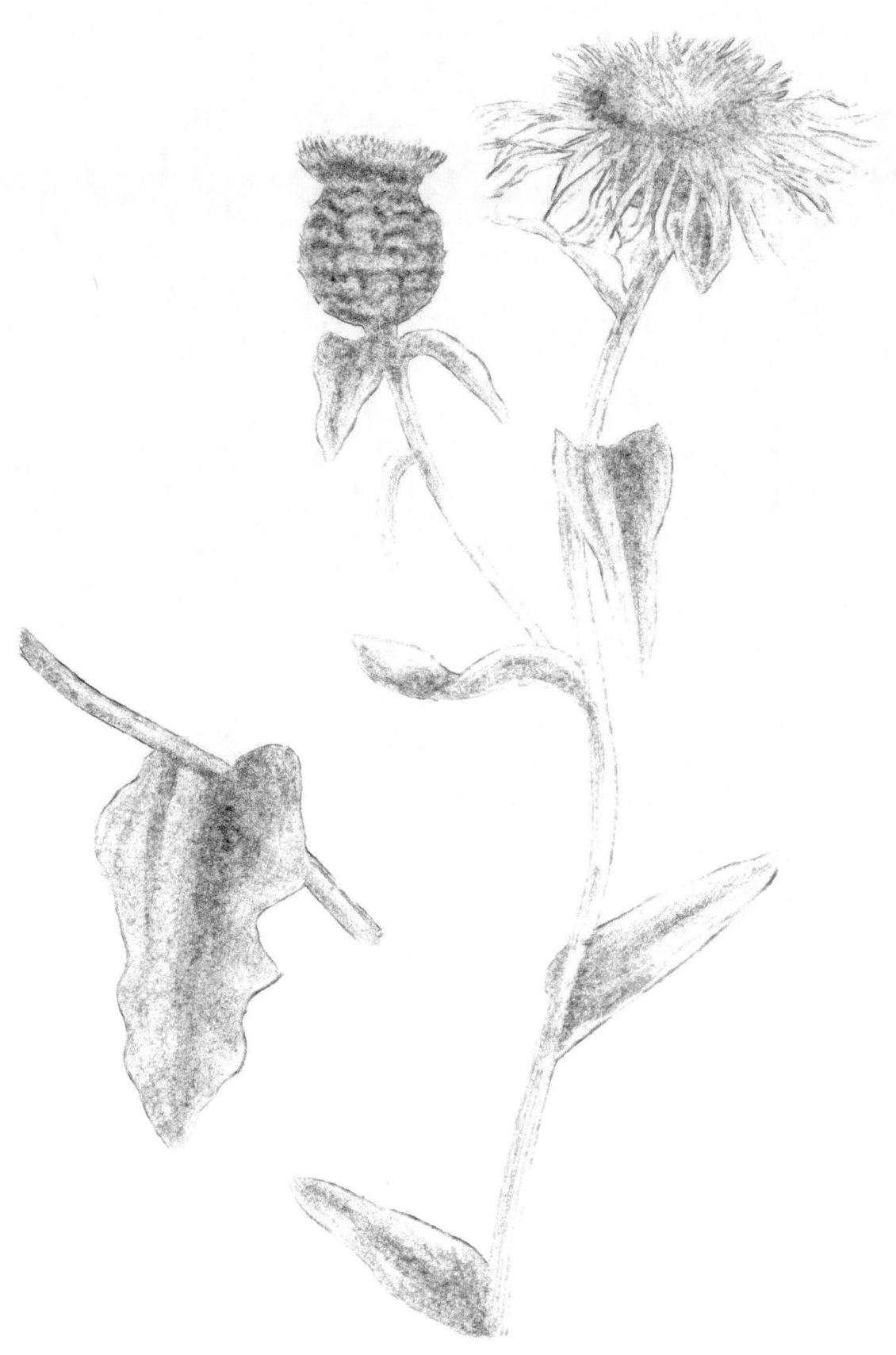

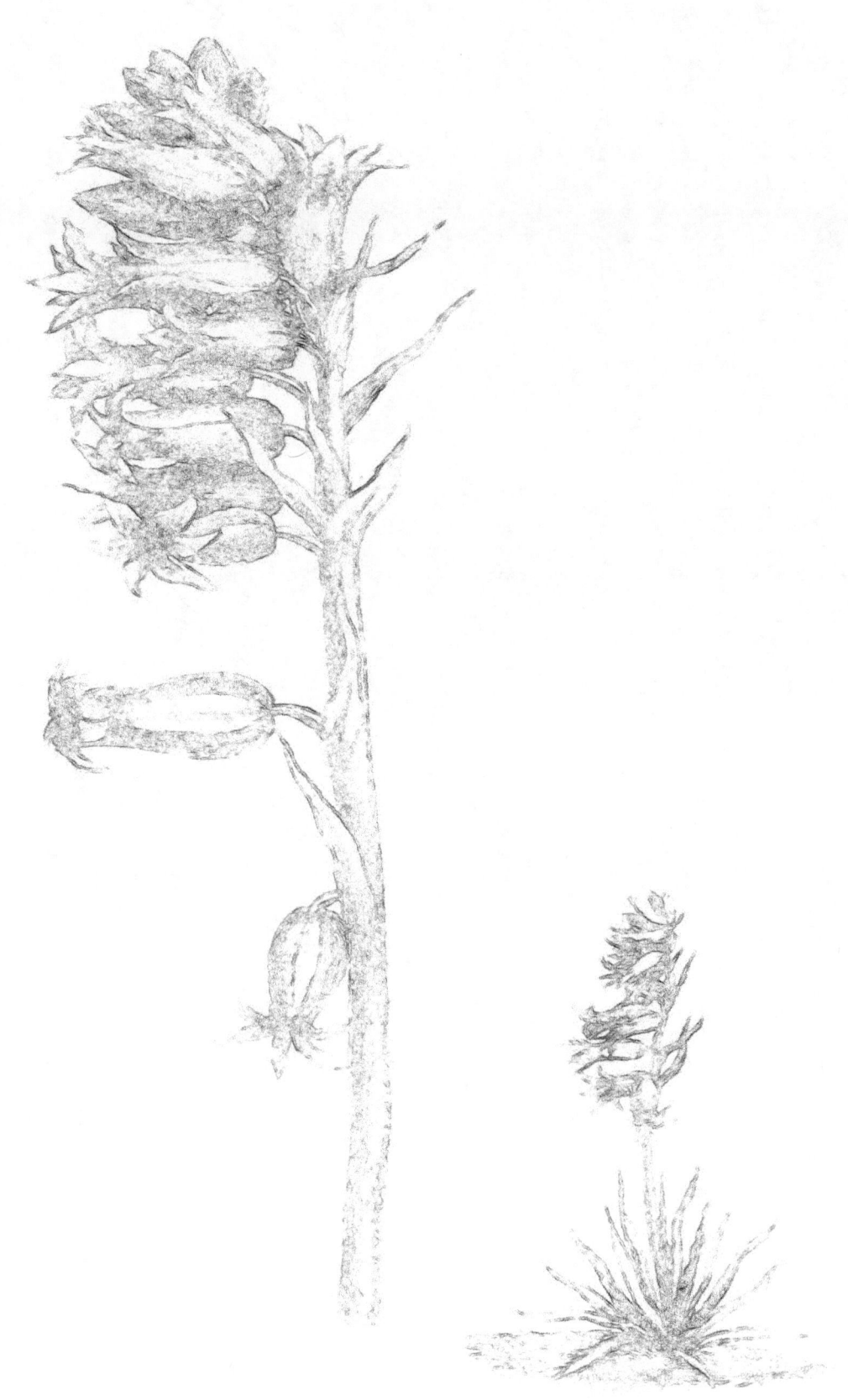

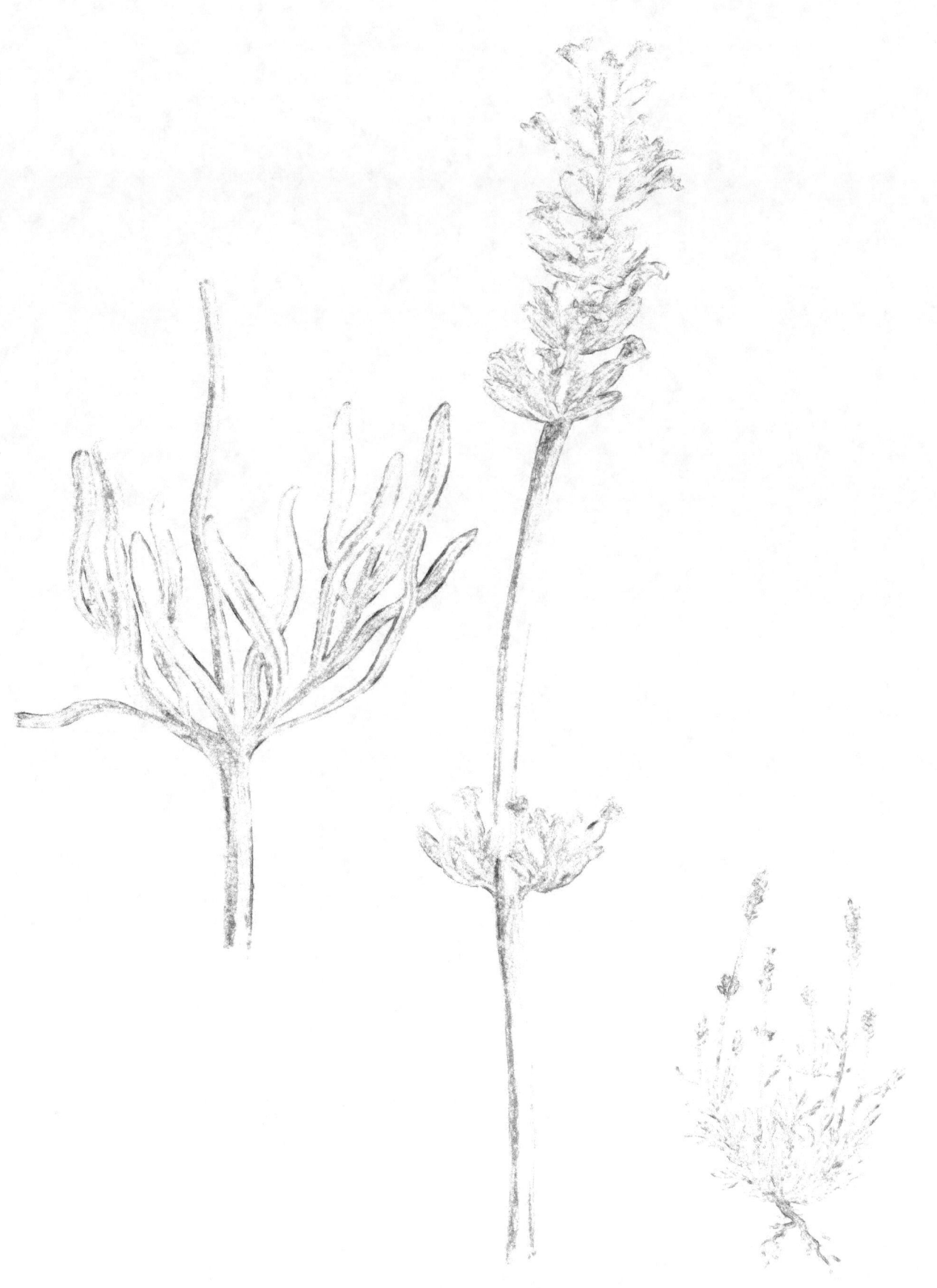

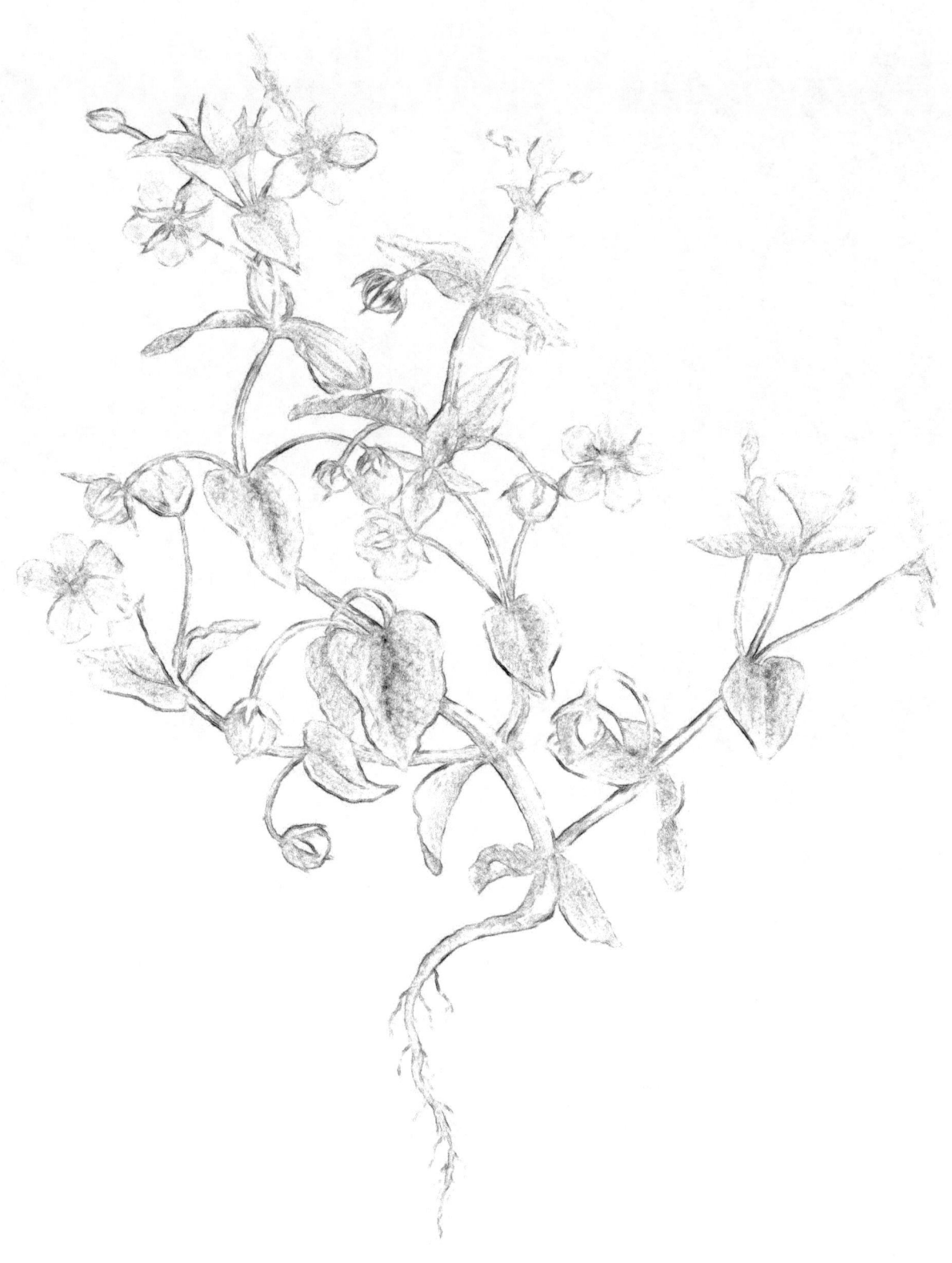

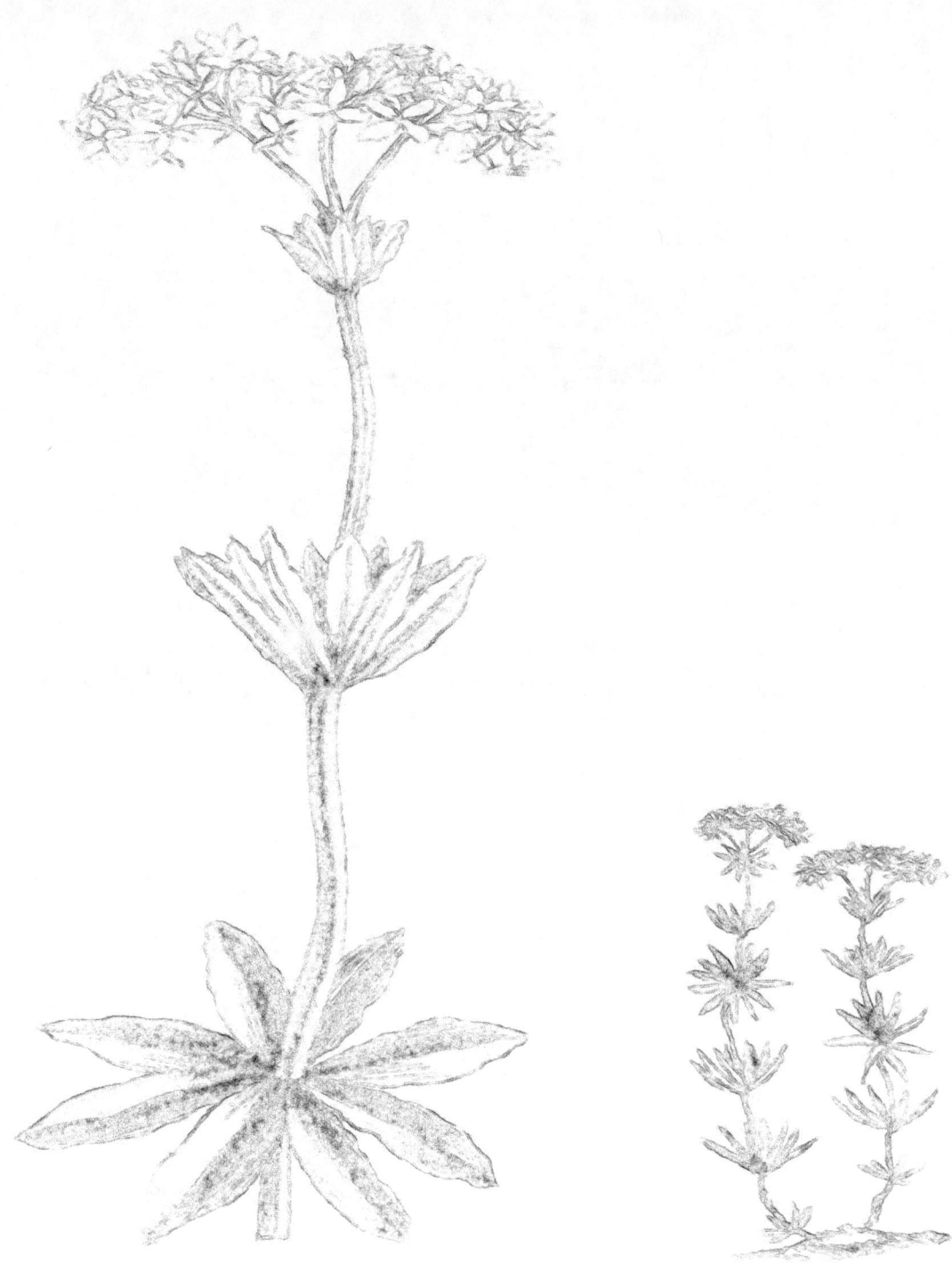

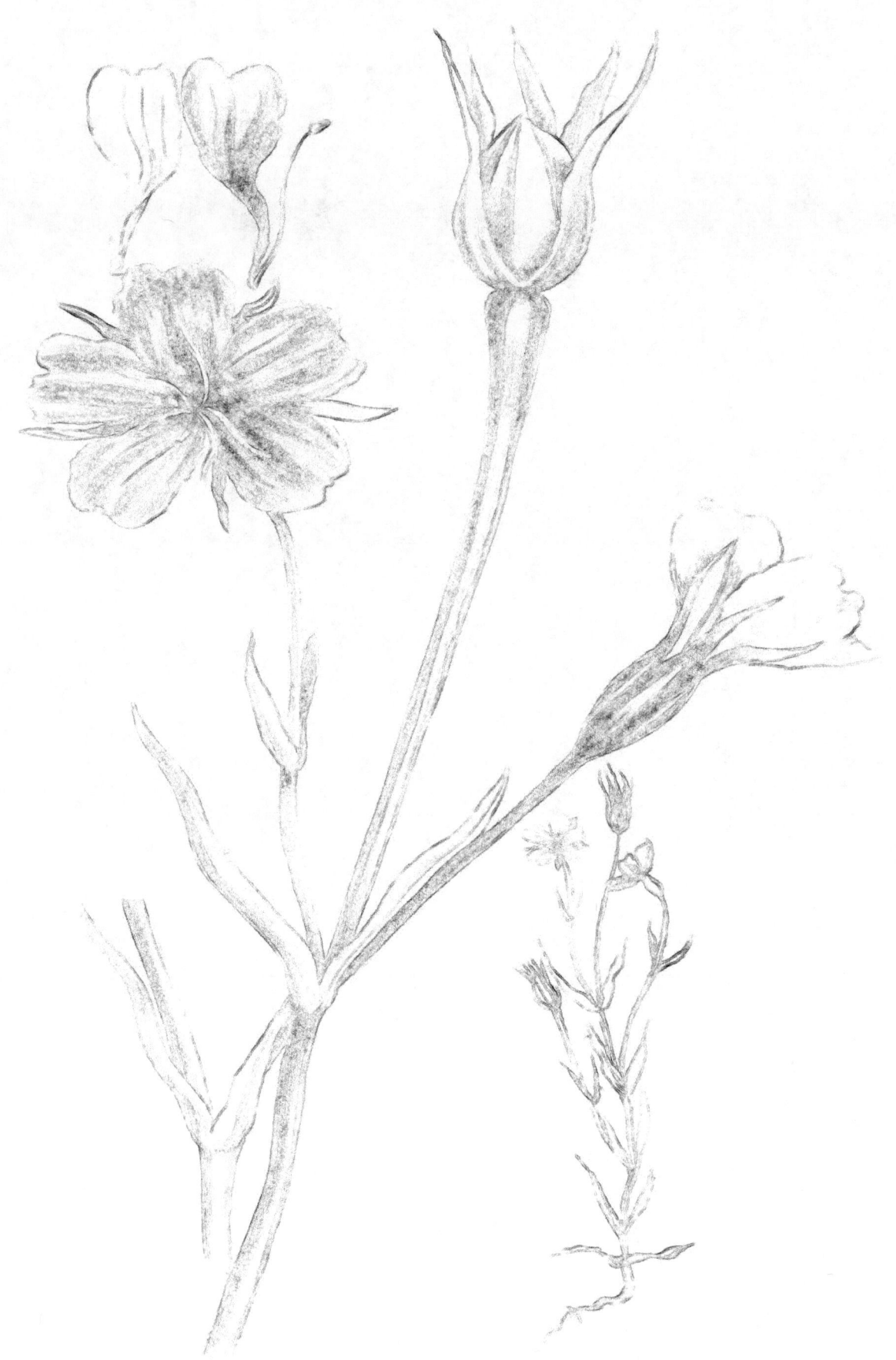

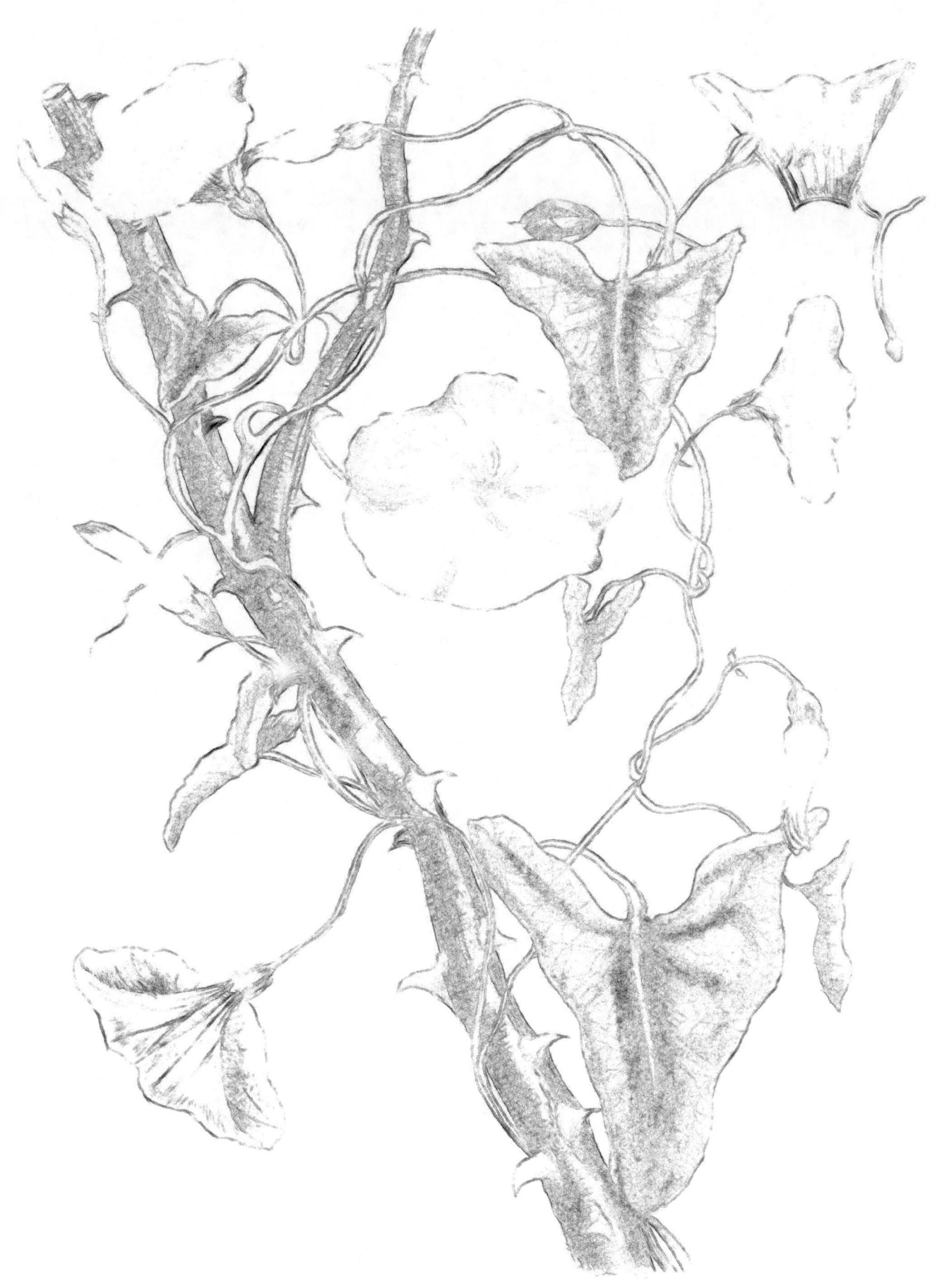

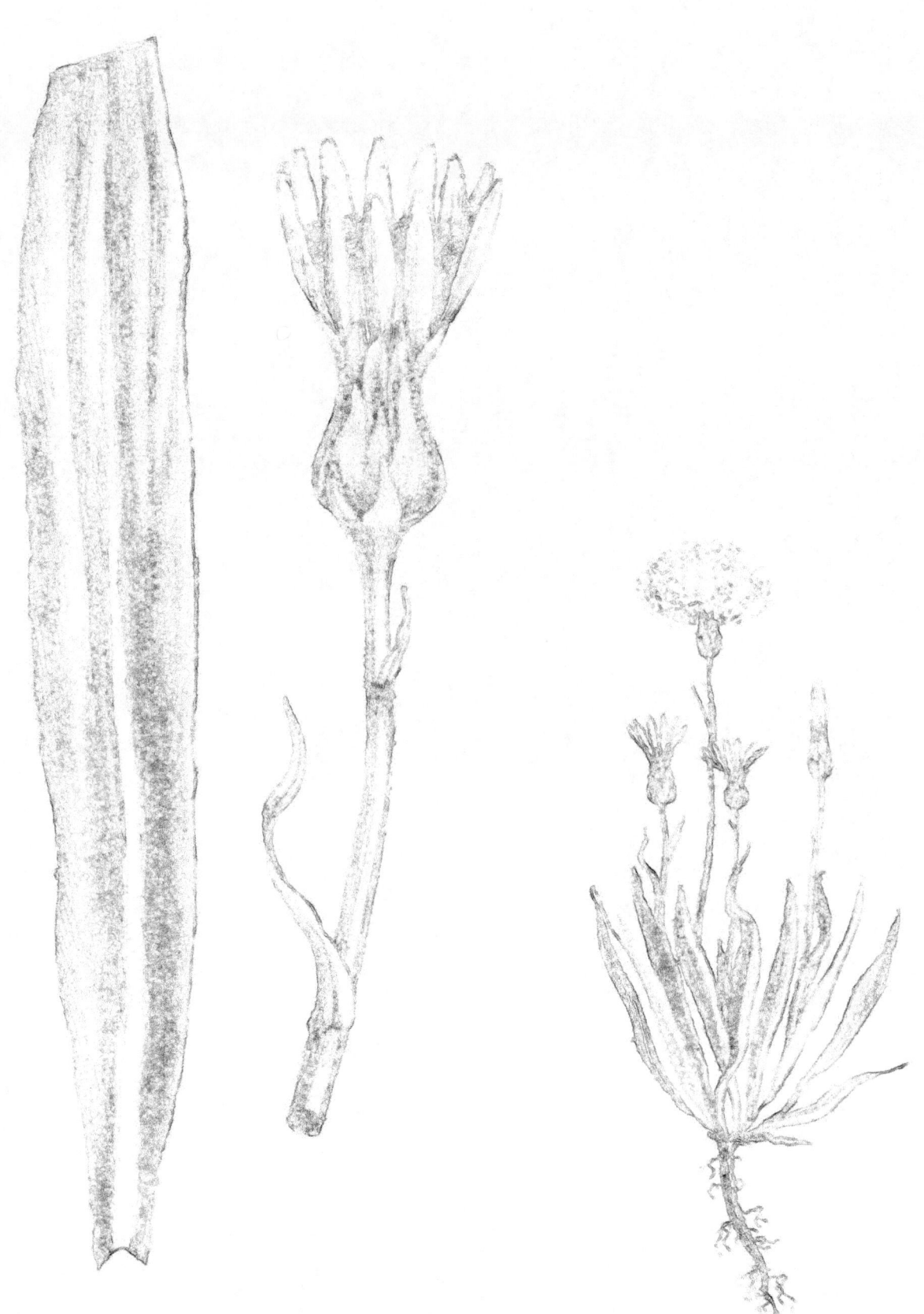

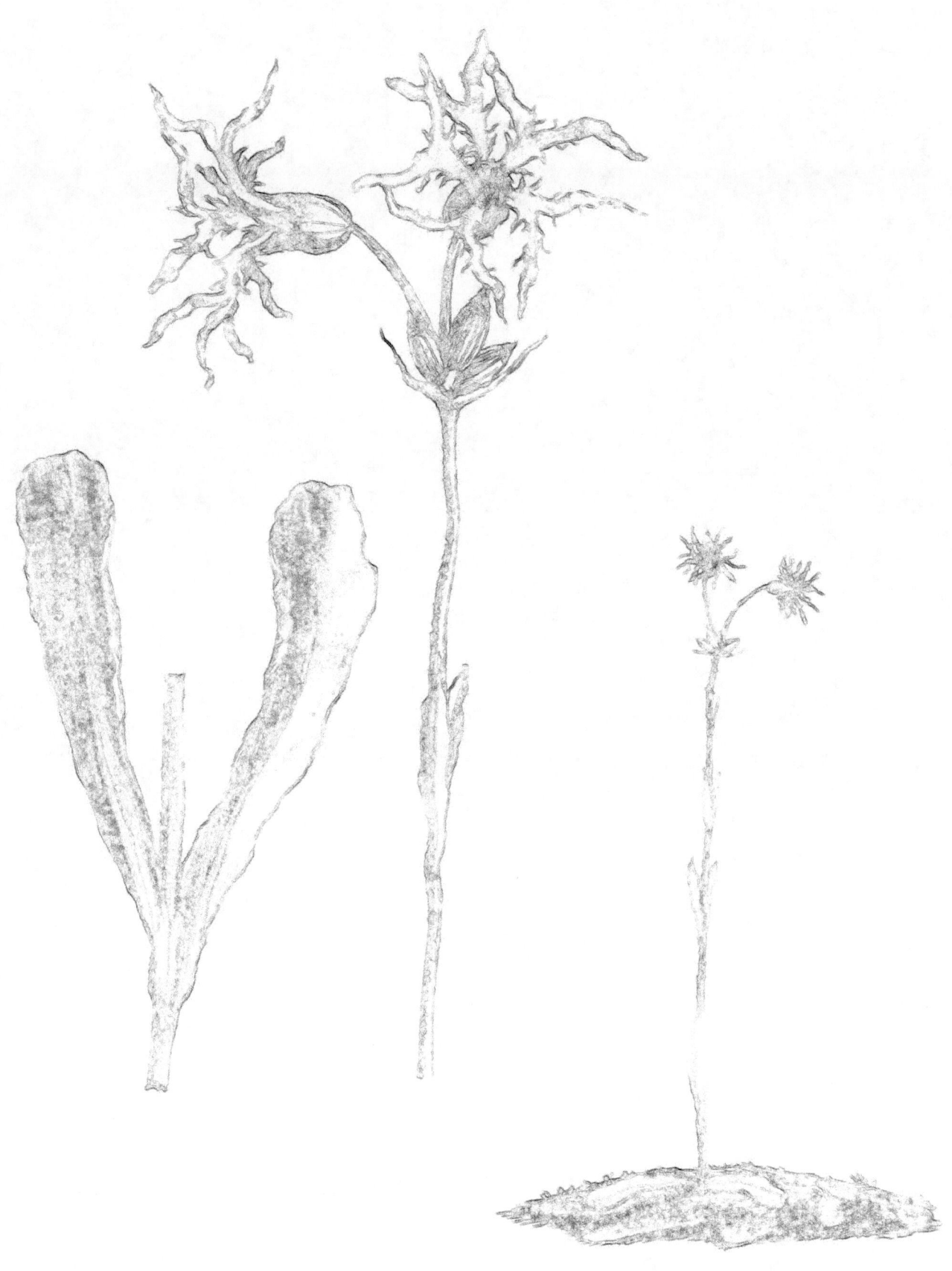

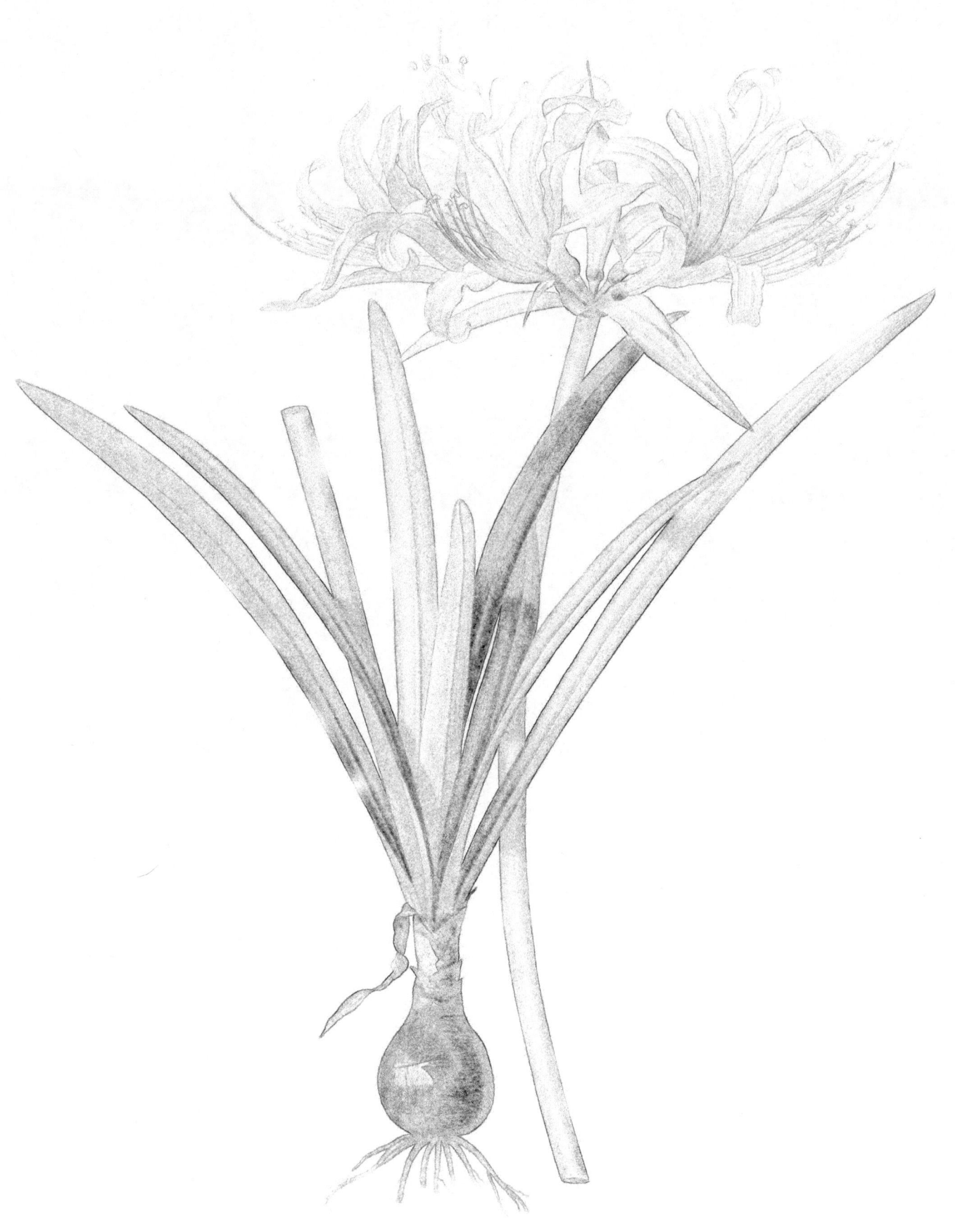

www.ingramcontent.com/pod-product-compliance
Lightning Source LLC
Chambersburg PA
CBHW080613180526
45168CB00007B/2892